Rose Oak

—

Behzad Jamshidi

Printed in the United States of America

ISBN 978-1-09833-121-4

Front cover image by Sarah Boisjoli
Book design by Behzad Jamshidi

First printing edition 2020.

Book Baby Publishing
7905 N. Crescent Blvd
Pennsauken, NY 08110

www.mooshnyc.com

My outstanding gratitude...

To Sarah Boisjoli, for lending her art to my story.

-

To my mother & father, who believed that I may one day have something important to say.

-

To my cousin Ali, for talking me down from trees, out of cities, and everything in-between.

-

To Zach – I'm sorry. So very sorry.

About Rose Oak

"Rose Oak" captures every part of our braveries, our fears, our regrets, our turmoil, our pains, and our hopes - planted at the roots of a single rose. This collection of poems incites themes that make us feel inadequate and ill equipped. Understanding our fears is a journey intended to make us stronger. For without our roots, we'd thirst and dry. Without our leaves, we'd never sway. Without our thorns, we'd be otherwise abused. Without our petals, we would never see ourselves as beautiful. Each piece of us, no matter the ache, works to serve a purpose. This is that story.

Roots

—

For what we thirst for, is who we are

I swam the tide of endless sea,
Searching for who I am,
Or what to be.
You cast your bait –
In greedy hate,
In hopes of it capturing me.
Upon that line,
It was me you find,
Struggling,
Dying,
Helplessly.
You looked into my eyes,
Beyond surprise,
That I stopped trying to struggle free.
You caught your prize
In those bubble eyes,
All the love in the world was there with me...
Upon an instant,
The breath of life,
I began to suffocate on air.
In a second instant,
I flapped my tail,
From the side of the rail,
And slipped back into the sea.
For I am a fish,
And my...
...
...
...
Three second memory
Dis-alludes their face from me,
But under scales,
Between the ribs perplexed to my skin
Like thread through fabric
Is the bait which lured me.
Incapable of passing past my throat,
Like a lump it bellows,
For loss to a fish is hard to swallow.
And every day,
You cast your line

At a similar time,
Picking fish like flowers from the soil of the sea.
Feeling rough scales,
Holding soft tales -
Staring into kind eyes.
I look up to see,
The top of the sea,
I am convinced you are heaven
Because you are above me.
And I,
Below your reach,
Force air out of my lungs
Until my belly rises to the top of the sea,
Just to realize that you are nowhere in sight to be.
In open sky,
I slowly die,
To the thought of you having replaced me...

Confessions Of A Monster

Fairy tales are when we whisper gentle comfort to our hearts,
And use colors to paint pretty pictures, not lessons.
Every part of life blue when my favorite color is green,
And my lessons were drawn in whatever my mother's favorite color was,
Back when she saw life in color.
Before the consequences of another's greed inspire grayscale.
Maybe a giraffe is just a horse
Who grew to ignore what was in front of them.
To raise their perspective.
Maybe grief is not as deep as they say,

As then I only truly see love in two things.
The way a child's eyes speak when they cannot,
And when a loved one is missed by their once love,
Because no landline can call The Fade.
And often enough, The Fade is not as far as they say –
The mind hosts peculiar places.
Rehearsed speeches of love that are as well shared to park squirrels
As then anyone.
My niece likes unicorns,
Though she does not even know it yet.
And my father lost something
Once upon a time.
And found it he did.
A pocket watch,
Two strings,
And a single thread of saffron.
As for far more did he search
In the corners of stranger's couches.
Unnecessary, unending –
Funny the many ways people beg.

Did you know that the average squirrel
Loses almost eight out of the ten acorns he finds?
Because within his greed
He cannot remember where he buried his jewels.
As I am trying to recover my mother,
As my father has forgotten where he buried her.
Possibly under a hill, with a quaint shadow?
Or more possibly within the cracks

Between the cushions of strangers couches,
Eight, maybe even ten acorns ago.

For only in sleep am I given everything I have ever wanted,
I dream giraffes and wake up to horses.
And horses are fair animals, but to some,
Of no questionable compromise
For the perspective of a giraffe,
Could help her possibly see where those acorns were buried.
As than a dream is an open sky where pennies could fall.
But you must be awake to collect them.
And pennies do not fall out of the sky,
We beg for those things on street corners and such.
To my niece,
May you learn your lessons in whatever colors you wish,
May you always dream of unicorns,
And wake up one day to realize you are one.
For you are no horse to be worked and ridden,
No giraffe forced into grief.
No squirrel to misplace her acorns,
But something so much more beautiful entirely.

We Are All Animals

Amongst sand box sorrows,
And dried juice to the right corner
Of my throbbing upper lip.
As you are every little bit of what did not kill you.
You are everything; everything it left you with,
Awesome ache and all.
As often,
What is not there,
Stolen toys by a venomous child,
Matter as much as what was.
For I've heard Bullies get theirs,
Sometimes.

Poison His Juice Box

Losing someone to the silence is similar completely
To the unending heartbreak of a piano key
Left only half played;
Soft touched, relished half-hearted –
What a shame to live life only partly brave.
The space between the strings and the air,
A temporary home where maybe whistles could live?
As a note is as deep and vast to fit the entirety of a very large small lake; Cold
weight and all – considering it is wintertime in Michigan.
And given both circumstance and opportunity,
Within that silence, that ocean,
I would most certainly drown myself.
Because we were not taught from books
As to how one keeps their head above the silence.
Algorithms, though useful, make poor flotation devices.
And though, when a moment has passed,
No key can quite fit the spaces unfilled with such scarcity,
As then, it may prove more important to be loud,
To make sound,
Than to be silent.
They are merely complete pieces of a moment without heartbreak,
For furry sounds of everything and nothing.
This, and only this,
We learned.

A Root, A Third, And A Shame

Be Not Brave,

For bravery is a golden allen key,
Capable of unlocking the truths in me.
Bravery is an effervescent light,
The ones we turn on before bed at night.

For bravery is speaking what lingers in thought,
Bravery is a soul that cannot rot.
Bravery is a light that finds love in despair.
Bravery is neither here nor there.

Bravery is what makes mad men seem right,
Bravery is as much virtue as might.
And though a coward it seems that you are,
From bravery, you linger not so far.

As bravery is a choice of ethereal mind,
We speak it, we feel it, we seek it, we find.
And of anything I'd take with me to the grave,
It is to say that you chose to be brave.

For bravery conquers the battle,
Bravery is clarity amidst the rattle,
And a fighter could rage & win not,
If he lived and fought only in thought.

And true men dive from arcadian sky,
Truth is no place good men should die,
But a man I suppose, you are not either,
And then so less a worthy fighter.

But if perhaps one is to be brave,
No regrets will haunt your grave,
As life will prove to be passionate Perth,
And bravery helps to prove your worth.

But be not brave,
For brave you are not.
Rest easy, kind coward,

Sleep well in plot.

And I hope one day,
You learn to be brave,
For a coward is only,
A spoken thought away.

But be not brave.

Brave, You Are Not

For all the flames within me you never lit.
For the consuming habits you never quit.
For "darlings" that should not have been spoken.
For every smile that kept my thoughts unspoken.
For every wish I saw crumble from the tips of stars.
For the foolish notion that this life was ever ours,
For every place, I wished to take your love,
For my self-pity that you think you're above.
For all those more gorgeous better fit for my grace,
For I am beyond you, for you hold no place.
For I no longer wish for you to be here,
For I am consoled, for I see clear.
For this is not you, that I need to get over,
For your memory died long ago,
Without a single, more-over.
For I am a stone unturned by your affection,
For this doting heart no longer does beckon.
For these emotions, just recently occur.
For all the things I thought you were.

For All The Things I Thought You Were

Leaves

—

A choice in life, is the bravest thing a man can make

Young heart, how dare you fall in love?
Such haste and insincerity will get us hurt!
Dear heart, do you heed not the warnings?
Pain is sure to come yet you still tread forward.
Love out of reach of stretching hands,
Patience being sanded down by time.
Young love, you do not yet know how to grow dear.
We shall pour water at your roots,
Watch your fruits slowly flourish.
Oh forsaken love, you plan to destroy us!
To leave us with less than that of which we had before.
You give love a face as if that should prove its worth?
You give love a voice to poison our conscious with feeble words;
You give love flesh and bone –
To hold us and to shake us from this eternal dream,
Only to wake up to a more infinite heaven.
Oh love,
Oblivion awaits, but agreed,
That she is no better way to get there.

Youth & Oblivion

Passion burns
Like thin leaves,
Kissed gently,
Consumed,
Ablaze.
Like the apprehensive young lovers learning
To exchange words without speaking for the first time.
It bends and curls -
A ritual dance in honor of love,
Possibly spite even.
It condenses down into itself
Cradleland child of love and wonders,
A frisson in honor of the moon & sun.
Lost lovers whose stories are public libraries.
And vulnerability is wanting to touch the
Very thing which you know could lick your skin off with fire & hate,
But the green expression is far too great not to be had.
And even in brumal cold is passion still more than logs burning.
Winter song is short and long,
But passion's chorus is forever louder.
As we know of many things,
But of this,
The many know nothing.

Winter's Journey

Autumn's leaves, brown and gray,
Fall darkness, dawn and day,
Gentle whispers from the fray,
May beauty be what leads your way.

For Autumn sings a hefty chorus,
Love in all it finds, Aquarius or Taurus,
Welcomed friends of aurous,
For beauty's leaves are all colors of forest.

Red as wrath, and green as plenty,
Yellow as the stars that sad men envy,
Beyond the temperance of gentle rain,
And deeper than the season's turning pain.

Summer was a life ago, the turning brittle heat,
Where laughter skewed faces; sadness void lead.
But there were needs for Autumn's rains,
To brush our gentle skin,
To embrace chilling oceans,
So that new life could begin.
For some leaves choose to be boisterous and brown,
And green to them is happiness not found,
And red though more brown than green,
Is still no place that Autumn seemed keen.

And star rays do find all those who look back,
For beings amongst a Caspian black,
Means beauty amalgamates more intact.
As I've never seen yellow buds blossom within the green,
Until Autumn's gentle rains did fall
And wash away that summer
To leave said flowers seen.

Because no season can start without another's end,
Though all are rather tame.
For the trees of Summer are that of Winter's,
But without all of Autumn's pain.
And the leaves of Autumn are one of color,
For it felt life to be lame.

As the world is iridescent -
Nature has intended as such,
So from the skies I call on the rain.
Wash off this land, the burden before,
Turn folly straight to ripe,
Diminish this darkness,
This foolish night
And bring us the star's day and light.

For never have I seen either flower or star
Shine so bright as a part of the black.
For Autumn's power is then this,
That her soul will shower;
Rejoiced in natures pact.
That true beauty lives where you choose to see it
And happiness lives in those words as so,
That in order for the Shepard to find its Nymph,
Shakespeare must also catch his doe.

As life is the chase to live beauty far longer,
Then age will allow it so,
But the shades of our soul,
That bends to our spines,
Are the textures of love we grow.
And a leaf is more beautiful having fallen
From trees where they cascade from green to gray.
Because what we are is seldom important -
For happiness watches as passion plays,
For a flower would never have been yellow
If it always chose to stay gray,
And the black Caspian would consume the forest,
If it did not give birth to the day.

As a season without passion,
Is no wind to sky to blow,
This I trust that Autumn know.
And her gentle kisses, green, grey or brown,
Will be the vaccine to all her sorrows.
And take this Autumn, I trust in you,

Do right by the forest's trees,
Grow any flower,
Color any bud,
But do not dare to forget me.
For your bravery has marked,
The start of a season,
Whose leaves will always shadow thee.

Her Name Was Autumn

Unfailing moon, you are mine,
Above this earth so divine,
For cast in a world of haste and hate,
You beckon us men with lunar bait.

And below your reach; a sea of sorrows.
Odd men and fish contempt tomorrows.
But nothing quite like this blessed day,
To cast thy troubles, far away.

For vermilion heavens float above,
The sky was kissed by obsidian love.
As no contempt can fracture thy,
In view of your aliquant alumni.

They dance the dark of your wedding suite,
A bride met tomorrow with ash and root.
For her flower was first from tempest shower,
To hold all life, the eternal bower.

Hanging within a brilliant blissful blue,
Iridescent blessings cast up to you.
For man knows not the way of air,
And less than so of celestial care.

But thy God put trust in I and thee,
To one day inspire a glimpse and see,
Unfailing moon, though you were mine,
No lunar bride was more divine.

Unfailing Moon

It scares me, you know?
Between this lust,
Between this doubt like honey between fingertips
That make handshakes awkward nasty things.
Or hugs that press into my neck like splinters.
Sheet metal lips,
Dry wall promises,
Love as momentary as cocktail glass ice;
Old fashioned sorrows.
Ice or fire, most things melt -
All things end.
I should possibly stop reading Frost.
I am forever in this place where,
I either feel undeserving of this love,
Or that I somehow deserve more from it.
Who is in charge?
Where do I bring my food stamp like scars
To trade them for a love that's digestible?
Something nourishing.
Something wholesome.
How can one feast and still feel hungry?
How does one starve and still feel full?
I don't like this meal very much.
I think I better make up some dietary restrictions.
I won't be eating again very soon.

"I'm A Vegan"

I grieve for the lesser life.
I cry over spoiled fruit,
Rotten seeds,
Forgotten trees,
Dead leaves,
Wasted air,
Black lungs,
Lost captains,
The beautiful,
The not.
I grieve for the greater life,
Because before I grieved,
Every single day,
Every second,
Every thought,
I grieved not.

The Lesser Life

And to what effect does life become a glorious day,
Casted between a drowned ocean and a heavy sky.
To what effect, do birds struggle through their pilgrimage,
Because we chose to clip their wings.
Do fish find discomfort in their place we made,
Somewhere dangling in the aching sky.
As we find comfort taking turns,
Drowning ourselves in the bodies of this ethereal divine.
To what degree does pain fissure, like passionate furry hate -
Fire of Caspian black and tomorrows un-promised.
To what measure do we learn to hate,
And hate,
And hate,
And hate,
Till we cannot recognize what was love once more?
To the detriment of who do we wage a war?
Do we spoil our kingdoms?
Do we drown our men,
To a battle of unimaginable loss?
And of who do we consider,
When the victory clouds our judgement?
To call fair not the casualties of innocence,
Because in the battle for victory,
A heart is right in intent
As it is in righteous thought.
But the battle,
The war,
The seize,
The fire,
Assures that either will win not.
For victory is a dirty game,
The one where true lesser man do play.
And a lesser man I thought not to be,
And you so just the same.
But a single kingdom is this game we play,
One will have to conquer and win this day,
And I submit, because a king I hope to be never,
If this new Kingdom holds nothing for me.
As I'd rather spend an eternal day,
Clipped wing,

Drowned sky,
And seeking to no end,
Than to know that my spite,
My ethereal divine,
Drowned in these thoughts of victory.

Take My Crown

As Frost once contemplated ice and fire,
But a choice in his mind wavered tired,
That if your fate was left to my effect,
I'd burn you from every thought acquired.

I'd take Dybek's scythe and go to the field,
Where the joys of you then in soil does shield,
And harvest you cold from reed tip to root,
I'd hatefully leave every part of Earth keeled.

That if Shakespeare's Doe were to one day be,
Your once lustful eyes staring back at me,
I'd worship the cross with gentle folly fate,
And from my golden bow - shoot it at thee.

As the stars of Rumi, do shine, do glow,
Of the places they have lit, no man would know.
So my purpose would be to leave this earth,
To test a chance in celestial snow.

And Ginsberg's Manhattan must then now be,
A concrete tomb for an arrangement of me,
And if I were to see you at your place.
I'd burry that city into the sea.

As through a nightmare, Hafez sent a boy,
You were once the ingredients to joy,
But in your absent place, placid poison.
Your hate was the horse to my Kingdom Troy.

For I spoke once of a thoughtless war,
Where a kingdom fell, where love did bore.
And your hands were stained of the worst proof,
My helpless hate to weight at my core.

And a writer expresses what in life he wrought
He sells himself to the things he's bought,
What a shame to be dry of this forgiving currency.
For dealing in lies are worth less than you thought.

Forgiveness Is Currency

Thorns

–

For are thorns not then a form of protection?

I am a monster,
You may not agree,
This is why you are,
A better man than me,
Because when I see me,
That is all that I see.

Do You See What I See?

Finger tips pressed against Acadian skies,
Who sits with you through all your cries.
Piercing red embellished by sunsets,
Torn cold, lonely, through all your upsets.
There is a story told of both Sun and Moon,
And together they make a brilliant maroon.
But cast along the shores of day,
Is night far longer than night should lay.
For being the world to one's passionate plait,
Make mighty seem sightless when seen through loves sight.
As being both - a passionate lover
And a radiant sky,
Cannot co-exists if none do cry.
And turquoise heeds the hate of many,
For Turkish warriors are not of plenty.
And recently these thoughts do seem to appear,
To hold you close and have you near.
As your eyes speak of radiant thistle,
And songs on my lips do linger and whistle.
And I do seem to contract a particular rush,
Only evident when hidden in your balmy blush.
So seal this love amongst an ocean of teal,
And these feelings of lonesome will feel less real.
As a scarlet dress does suite you best,
And crying absent of laughter suites you less.
And forever this heart is where you lay,
But joining our love is antinomic at best.
For being a passionate lover and a radiant sky,
Is said not to exist if none do cry.
And I am but a simple moon,
Destined to be a lonely maroon.
And you are cast as Acadian sky,
I do hope one day your tears do dry.

China Doll

You left searching for breaths,
Like the faces of people,
I've never meet nor hope to ever see.
You are both my inability to express,
Onto the world these emotions;
A person I wish to someday be.
You hold me tangled in your words,
Like prisoners through barb wire,
Bleeding, dying, helplessly.
You are affixed into my notions,
Of both love and happiness,
A depravity of my longing affinity.
And I hope to god one day,
The one above or below,
That this dry, brittle longing will go.
For a life without love,
Is no water to an ocean,
No wind through sky to blow.
So I shall sing my chorus,
Aquarius or Taurus.
Love in all I welcome though.
Amantes sunt Amentes,
For I know your edges to be rough,
A sander of some kind we'll burrow.
But remember no love on earth,
Has ever touched the sky,
Without feeling a star's sorrow.
For burning bright and beautiful,
Amongst a Caspian black,
Is nor a thoughtful today or tomorrow.
But feeling the gravity from love,
And your kisses - bellow or above,
Will be the cure to all my sorrows.

You Left Me For Breaths

Never gone -
You are never gone,
Though you dwell
In the realm of which
Words cannot reach you.
No longer can your hands preach,
Ocean call of sunset and wake.
But from your passing,
There is much that you teach.
Much that we learn.
As life continues with one broken leg
Or one missing finger.
A ghost of what was once there.
Whole, unaltered.
Separated limbs much like your own,
But sadly ours more figurative.
Reborn, in visions of your smiles,
Like dying wishes granted on our life-beds.

Grace

In a humble abode somewhere in my heart,
Lives the love for you dismissed by our part.
I set fire to its walls, and watch as nothing seems to burn you,
I gust tempest wind and woe as nothing seems to turn you.
I bear crags upon your head and stand idle
As the roof c
        o
         l
        a
     p
   s
  e
d
But from under ruble,
Stretching hands,
You emerge
And I elapse.
I grow bitter and cold in hopes to stop my beating heart.
But the thoughts of you which I bear in my soul,
They warm me from end to start.
I spark a careless thought from within my soul,
Fury & desire to see you burn down into ash.
But my relentless hatred, and my never-ending love
For you will always clash.

Burning Houses For Fun

Where does one stand if not yet in the grave?
To live while dying is some form of brave.
Do they still feel the influx of summer's gentle air?
Do they still saunter through clouds, beyond worry and care?
Do they touch memories like yesterdays silk, or tomorrows velvet?
Do they still gasp at the wonder of the ethereal sunset?
Do they still heal wounds, from under their skin?
Or are they too busy planning a new life's begin?
Do lovers still feel something solemn and whole?
Where once a man did live, before life took its toll?
For dragonflies seek flowers, before life in life is done,
But life is sought to be over, even before life's' begun.
And how does the Shepard keep his band intact,
When one from their folly is cast and call to the second and final act?
How do then birds saunter gently admits the raging sky,
When brother, sister, father, and mother are all amongst who die?
And how does one then address their audience
At the in-audible end of their show?
We have all but a chance to be brilliant and beautiful,
From this,
From life
Is all I know.

La Libellule Des Flâner

These are bones,
They belonged to someone near to me.
They are the brittle fractures of a body
Which died fighting a monster -

He will no longer peruse around our beds,
Taking the light bulbs out of our nightstands
And smashing them on our heads,

With these bones you could twist the tips
And make a sword perhaps.
The ankles favor better
For pocketknives and envelope openers.
I have heard though once,
If you plant the bones where tulips grow,
The bones will spread roots and turn them into roses.

Far easier this way than to replant all those flowers.
As it also makes more time in the late afternoons for weapon making,
For a fighter never truly choses to be born,
But they sprout the first of their thorns regardless.

And I wonder if my mother searched for me ever –
Please send her letters.
I know she remembers where she planted my bones,
But does she know that I turned those tulips to roses for her?
Does she know that the rest of me lives elsewhere?

Darling, dry your tears.
Salt water does little for funeral flowers.
Mother,
I ache for you -

Always.

These Are Bones

I went to the heart of where I buried you.
I stuck my arms up to my elbows in the body of that guilt,
In the weight of that remorse,
In the cold affliction of ungodly secrets.
I bent at the mercy of your forgiveness,
Located somewhere between my heart and my spine.
I peeled petal,
Upon petal,
Upon petal,
Till the flower garden hissed at my careless crude contempt.
I stopped saying I was sorry,
And watched the first of my flowers grow.
I started putting a single drop of honesty
In every elixir I fed people for their sorrows.
I began reserving that love for those who would bow
And balance halos above their shadows.
I began to trust with freedom because I grew in these days
To be resistant to the infections of the heart.
I grew tolerant of the noise,
Irreverent to the pursuant natures of joy
That cost more than they were ever truly worth.
I went to the heart of where I buried you
To drown myself -
Not in guilt, but in ocean wake for what I have done.
I stuck my head heavy below that cold,
Waiting for forgiveness to fill my lungs,
For the somber chills to clench my ache.
And I heard a hiss from the dark deeps,
A voice eroded from your own.
I grew gills in that callous haste to be forgiven.
I heard your whisper,
Cold,
Clear –
"This is what it feels like to live with gilt.
Brave, honest - drowning.
Air is for those birds who have freedom fill their lungs,
You are a fish.
You are not that beautiful.
Love, this is what sorry feels like."
And with the air of those words,

In open sky,
I slowly die,
To the thought that -
You cannot come to forgive me.

Be Very Sorry

Petals

—

Grief inspires such beautiful colors

Tell me the "Once Upon A Time..."
Of how the Sun burned for the Moon with love.
Speak of their separation in distance
Like it is the most dismal detail between them.
That of a single love in this world so high,
The Sun is the only star in his empty sky.
And though floating aimlessly with racing rancor,
The Moon is the Sun's eternal anchor.
Profess of how the Sun and Moon make love,
Embracing each other in a solstice of beauty,
And an effervescent eclipse of their hearts.
Tell me the story of how the Sun died each night,
Just so that the Moon could live.
That there is nothing less than the world and life,
That to Moon, dear Sun, won't give.
Bibi Joon, tell me a story.

Bibi Joon, Salam

Come love, come love, come love.
For the space between us is vast,
For the green grows greener in grass,
For life takes fury too fast -
Come love, come love, come love.
So no judgment between us shall pass,
No two moments should forever last,
As burden is a weightless task -
Come love, come love, come love.
Life is a song spoken with no sound,
A road to walk with no ground,
A green tree destined to brown -
Come love, come love, come love.
When mercy's thirst falls on your day,
When life is a journey – no road, no way,
When thirst renders you with no speech, no say -
Come love, come love, come love.
And if earth serves you no longer,
No anchor here stronger,
A breath you cannot conquer,
To you,
Wherever you reside
In the great big world and wide -
I'll come love, come love, come love.

Come Love, Come Love, Come Love

Sometimes it seems more peaceful to sleep silent
Than to sleep a dreamer.
I close my eyes to imagine what normal looks like.
For in the end we are all bones,
And how then does bravery preserve us?
As skin is only the beginning –
What does your heart whisper to you?
Because no ember can every burn you,
Without having sparked a flame.
And no life worth living,
Can ever truly be lived,
If it had not persevered through pain.
We are all brave,
Yes.
And,
We are so much more than that.

Ineffable

I envy not the greater man, for I am every bit of bravery.
I am able to reach into my joy, fingers deep,
And summon it every time I smile.
I can hear myself at the lips of my voice,
There in heart, threaded through air and sound.
I am able to look upon myself, and recognize
That my world has gifted me a crown.
That my eyes do not see all colors,
Only those that are kind.
That I enjoy the ocean, the air of the sea,
Just as much as both everything and nothing.
That my skin is the greatest place to be,
That my bones no longer torture me.
That if I were to drop at worlds end,
There would be as many strangers there as friends.
I can reach into the sky, and with my will,
Pull every star to lend their light.
I am every bit better, and every bit stronger,
Because I have tasted every part of spite.
And a crown I wish not, to hold over my head,
The thrown I gave up long ago,
For I am no coward, for I am no man,
Who without love would call here home.
I put passion to this journey,
I put fight to this chorus,
I put purpose into the gifted day.
As I can dream once more,
And rest my eyes,
And know that I am all that and more.

What Is Your Purpose?

I dreamed a dream that dreamers dream,
One that lovers see obscene,
And those who dare tread un-keen,

I dreamed a dream that no one has seen.

For searching oceans on Lazarus's sight,
Is but not a true lover's passionate plait.
I heed thy fear with all my might,

I dreamed a fire that dare not light.

I dreamed a dream that dreamers deem,
One that men still feel too green,
And lovers still appear not keen,

I dreamed a courage as it seemed.

For fighting air will then choke true,
As does those things which broke through,
But challenge does provoke a many few,

I dreamed a dream that spoke you.

As that loving dream in you awoke,
In a burning house of hate and smoke,
Tragedies lessons; a soulless joke,

But the dare to dream it can invoke.

So when love finds you, let it in,
As passion heads no late begin,
And forever happiness is simple sin,

For dreamers too long it seems we've been.

As somnambulist do walk this earth,
And find love in immortal mirth,
For life's purposeful poised worth,

Is to carry a joy to one day birth.

For dreamers dream many dreams,
Until day is brought to night it seems,
Until tears gush like endless streams,

And purpose feels like silent screams.

Those dreamers make a mighty shake,
The need to be needed in souls do ache,
A life full and plenty, this does make,

To dream a dream by heavens sake.

As I dreamed a dream, I thought it was,
But atlas a dream it was not as so,
The Shepard did find his nymph,

And Shakespeare did catch his doe.

And this life has helped plenty more,
Than dreamers that have touched this life,
As with them came solemn and sadness,

And a great deal more of stupid-strife.

But not a single dream stayed a dream,
All lived in these words as so,
That where this worlds winds will carry,

Is not of places that men do know.

For I am a being living life as is,
Schooled here from a dreamer's day,
And amongst this grandness I find myself,

A place forever, where I shall then stay.

As I dreamed a dream that dreamers dream,
Just so that I may come to say,

No dreamers dream will deem more than dream,

Until dreamers, we prove not, one day.

I Dreamed A Dream...

Once was a home, of many did know,
A blue Jay nestled on a golden tree,
The graces of comfort, the mercies of winter,
The leaves of love fell free.
But a comfort at last, too good to last,
In spite of did blue Jay see,
A future in love, an ethereal above,
But all without the tree.

The tree bore winter, its hateful ascend,
The stalks were covered in snow,
The world gave no graces, no warm embrace,
To gloom was tree to go.
But the sun did sponsor, the day with wonder,
And melt away that snow.
And of its strength, of its unfailing roots,
To the forest a tree did show.

As spring sang its chorus, the bark grew porous,
The forest would then now glow,
For the roots of nurture, belong in common,
Of its welcome we all do know.
And so birds to no end, animals & friends,
To golden forest did show.
For aspirations of height, in root tip and stalk,
Live in the cold burden low.

And a blue Jay remembered, a beautiful September,
It graced onwards towards the tree,
Their journey for more, in hate did it bore,
No happiness then to see,
As in spite of our truth, our beautiful youth,
What is said about what we should be?
Proof has no worth, when sadness is sponsor,
For nothing in life then is free.

And so no space alas, for blue Jays of past,
For the things that have gone must go.
For granted grace, in empty space,
Is a miracle that few do know.

For this is a tree, a spire of greatness,
For those whom it houses do glow.
For high is this tree, this beauty we see,
Through the deepest of griefs did grow.

That the winds will call, leaves will grow and fall,
But a tree at last I will be.
For if there is no comfort or grace, no empty space;
Of my worth I will always see.
For the forest bore, no wage no war,
Just a home to welcome thee.
Of a many I have loved, both of earth and above,
But there is no home granted for thee.

For though a blue Jay, seemingly sweet,
Broad in stature,
In color then neat,
Still know not of, the graces above,
Taking peelings of tree bark in beak.
Should be aware of that vanity, of disrespectful profanity,
To all love it does then meet.
And the forests speaks, so the blue Jay seeks,
No home to welcome or rest his feet.

For etched in me, are the comforts which see,
A past that is just that,
So if I am a bird never, it would be a better forever,
To walk this earth then as rat.
For though oppressed & tired, against conspired,
A cold dark place I was at,
But triumph in spite, of the griefs of life;
For is there a better existence than that?

Blue Jay, Blue Jay - Go Away

Fortune smiles at many a man,
Those whom gravity cannot bend,
Those whom weather storms unmoved,
Those whose dreams contest yet proved.

For a simple soul, within a cell will rot
As chains and darkness leaven the heart,
But a haunted soul will always aspire,
For when life heeds floods, said souls soar higher.

For more than a day has my life been a storm,
And more than dreams from this life have been torn,
But a jagged edge does craft a great weapon,
And the fury to fight in this heart does beckon.

As no reed in river has yet to be moved,
No sturdy rock to stone not smoothed,
No burden in life left not improved,
As from burdens we find ourselves removed.

For a dreamer and a fighter in night in-lay,
To thoughts of such a glorious day,
That a dollar they cannot, in subtext pay,
Though the dreamer and fighter still bought the day.

And fortune smiles, though we see it not,
Happiness holds both faces & thoughts,
And simple is simple when given all is heart,
This gravity of emotions; must we soon depart.

For think of how we ponder the rain,
And thunder beckons and sings to our pain,
That if these emotions we too could tame,
Success in life, could be as simple as rain.

We collect our parts, offer them to the air,
Allow them to store somewhere safer and fair,
And we rise gripping claim to the bower,
Tempest storm of thunder and shower.

We awaken every fiber of our sempiternal parts,
The ones that stem and cross our souls with our hearts,
And every escapade relished – a tapestries of arts,
For when life ends is when it truly just starts.

And even the coffin oak is soaked from the rain,
And so I will dissolve without fury or pain,
For I, was the river, I tread forward in spite,
No dam to dam dare to challenge my might.

For fear this silent soul,
His life has taken a toll.
But of a single change he'd make not,
For in no coffin he would wish to rot.

For when life has no way,
Call to your clouds and say,
"The fearless do not quiver.

The rains will fall and make me a river.

And with that river every wall will fall,
I will follow the stream deep and tall,
For do not tell me it is impossible per say,
I am the rain,
I am the river,
I will carve my own way."

Fortune Smiles

I lay awake,
Nestled,
In cold burden earth.
Coffin oak stirring the aromas of geraniums and tulips –
They never did know my favorite flowers.

I thought to myself...
This cold,
It does ill upon my fighter bones,
That I should lay here not,
A dream was wrought,
A life yet in stone I shall foster not.

So I awoke -
As simple as light comes to day,
Though clouds, cloud and warry the way,
And wonton rain in tempest falls,
But the day is still the day,
And way leads on to way.

I planted feet to the yellow woods,
And road the path
Which the wind stirred as I stood,
The smell of rose and tulips,
To meet one day - it should,
So both roads would fair me just the same.

I trip and fell,
The road from hell,
Ever root had knot in front of me.
But still I cried,
The fighters sigh,
This road I'll ride,
To state I tried.

For coffins are an atelier for dreams,
And dismal-brave life may seem,
But a burden in me was that dream.
To leave feeling felt, but otherwise unseen.

I live off the soil,
Whatever spoils,
The forest brought to me that day,
And I fought to wander,
The light of day,
That the place I was,
I had no desire to stay.

And within this will,
Was that man I'd kill,
Sorry not for in the coffin he wished to rot.
And upon that burden path,
Was more beauty and laugh,
Lavish and love,
Gentle gifts surely from something above.

For every rock which vexed my fall,
Every burden which spoke and call,
Had a flower of ethereal beauty meet it just the same.

As than life is this,
To love and miss,
To return in empathy of those you will and know.
And so,
Two paths diverged in a yellow woods,
The better claim played on my will not,
For a journey of any kind was what I sought.

And how way leads on to way,
I can now come to say,
That the difference was already made.
For out of the coffin my flower did sprout,
It did make that garden,
A miracle through doubt.

And the yellow woods gave way to those yellow stars,
Which like the wiser men than men,
I followed them through the road to the bend.
And upon my eyes,
Beyond surprise,

Was I brought yet to the claim I sought in life.
And just as the fighter,
My weapon is pointed,
My brush is the craftsman's knife.

And until the coffin calls me back,
And hopes to hold me once more,
This road I have burdened,
This path I have left,
Will be all the joy for I to adorn.

And when my place is brought
Back to that cold,
I will have by then proposed.
My favorite flower is the rose,
For though thorns spite its valiant pose,
All beauty in life
Is ridden with spite,
The things you will most will forever have those.
And one day they will be telling this with a sigh,

Somewhere ages
And ages
And ages hence –
Two roads diverged in a woods and I –
Took the one which the wind spoke,
Lifted me out of my grave,
Cascade storm of rose and oak,

As this is a story of resilience,
And that my dear,
Has made all the difference.

Rose Oak

Roses

—

For healing is a journey that not all wounds seek

A snake did lead Eve away from Eden,
What a pity, us things, are always needing.
And hate is at the truth of all resolve,
The root to of this happiness, I've yet to solve.
For once did these skies carry glory,
For once these lips did speak a story,
A moment only in this shameful life,
Did things seem different, did things feel right.
And a bite from an apple seemed sinful not,
For what now dwells, both in mind and in thought.
I am a human, I am made like no tree,
I cannot shed my leaves and still be me.
I cannot thirst for an eternal day,
Until rain is brought to my helpless way.
And I've spent far longer on what I am not
Than after that person I've both loved and sought.
For I am no dreamer, and a fighter less so,
I am no prize, no Shakespeare's doe.
I am no sun, no earth, no moon,
I am neither black, nor maroon.
I fail beauty from a deep-rooted place,
For I fear this earth, no home, no space.
But I forfeit my grief so long ago,
When the first of my things did go.
And with her life I became a lesser man,
Who claimed less then to the burden land.
So I dream through others, I give to thee,
The things I could not for myself then be.
And if happiness finds itself on a moment so,
Then for that I will stay - alas no go.
And I swear by this life to do it all better -
I hope to live again never.

For Eve Left Eden

Then destiny sees,
In eternities lips,
The most divine decline to atrophy.
Will I then be,
As pretty as those leaves
When I jump out of this tree?

Tell Me I'm Pretty

About The Author

—

Behzad Jamshidi is a Canadian born artist who specializes in story telling through several mediums. Jamshidi is primarily a Chef, working as the Executive Director of a cultural organization devoted to the development of socially conscious projects and businesses called Moosh. Jamshidi's Iranian background and exposure to both art and poetry from an early age inspired him to use the power of dialogue to create moments of empathy through all the various social experiences he curates. After abandoning formal education for literature & writing after high school, Jamshidi took a journey abroad, through Europe and the United States in order to better situate his culinary career.

Through a chronic, life threatening illness, loss, and the difficulties of maintaining mental health, many of the themes that he has felt are less positioned as food driven narratives find their place in his poetry. By long influence of Robert Frost, Alfred Lord Tennyson, Rumi, Hafez and others, Jamshidi appreciates using certain classic elements of literature and poetry to thoughtfully capture difficult personal narratives. This is Jamshidi's first complete published piece, marking a transition into more transparency, honesty, and authenticity.

At the core of his poetry is resolve and hope that experiences will challenge us, break us, and irrefutably give us agony, but enable us to become something stronger than we were — if only we are willing to let it. Jamshidi's currently splits his time between projects in New York and Los Angeles, working to foster more projects to impact our communities across America, validate social conscious creators, and carry narratives that aspire to make the United States a more inclusive country for all.